★★★★★
MLB TEAMS

Milwaukee BREWERS

KENNY ABDO

Fly!
An Imprint of Abdo Zoom
abdobooks.com

abdobooks.com

Published by Abdo Zoom, a division of ABDO, P.O. Box 398166, Minneapolis, Minnesota 55439.

Printed in the United States of America, North Mankato, Minnesota.
102025
012026

Photo Credits: AP Images, Getty Images, Shutterstock
Production Contributors: Kenny Abdo, Jennie Forsberg, Grace Hansen
Design Contributors: Candice Keimig, Neil Klinepier

Library of Congress Control Number: 2025936778

Publisher's Cataloging-in-Publication Data

Names: Abdo, Kenny, author.
Title: Milwaukee Brewers / by Kenny Abdo
Description: Minneapolis, Minnesota : Abdo Zoom, 2026 | Series: MLB teams | Includes online resources and index.
Identifiers: ISBN 9798384940241 (lib. bdg.) | ISBN 9798384941002 (ebook) | ISBN 9798384941385 (read-to-me ebook)
Subjects: LCSH: Milwaukee Brewers (Baseball team)--Juvenile literature. | Baseball teams--Juvenile literature. | Professional sports--Juvenile literature. | Sports franchises--Juvenile literature. | Major League Baseball (Organization)--Juvenile literature.
Classification: DDC 796.357--dc23

Table of CONTENTS

BREWERS

Since 1970, Wisconsin's Milwaukee Brewers have brewed up big plays, star players, and big moments for fans. In the land of cheddar, this team proves that baseball is always on the menu!

22

YELICH
22

The Brewers are built on strong players, smart leadership, and loyal fans. With Hall of Famers and power hitters, Milwaukee brings the flavor to the field!

BATTER UP!

The Brewers began in Washington State in 1969 as the Seattle Pilots. After one season, the team moved to Milwaukee and became the Brewers just six days before Opening Day. Even on short notice, a crowd of more than 37,000 showed up for Milwaukee's opening game on April 7, 1970.

S

Milwaukee
19

In the early years, the Brewers worked to improve. In 1978, the team had its first winning season with 93 wins. By 1980, shortstop Robin Yount led a strong lineup that hit over 200 home runs. The team was starting to brew up something special.

In 1982, the Brewers had a strong season, winning the **American League** (**AL**) **pennant**.

The team reached the World Series but lost to the Cardinals in seven games.

GRAND SLAMS

The Brewers had ups and downs over the next few years. In 1987, Paul Molitor hit safely in 39 straight games, one of the longest streaks in Major League Baseball history. Yount reached 3,000 career hits in 1992. In 1998, the Brewers moved to the **National League (NL)** to begin a new chapter.

In 2000, the Brewers welcomed slugger Richie Sexson to the lineup. In 2001, the Brewers got a brand new stadium. That season, Sexson hit 45 home runs, one of the highest totals in Brewers history.

In 2008, the Brewers made the playoffs for the first time in 26 years. Prince Fielder's power and CC Sabathia's pitching helped clinch the **NL wild-card** spot. In 2011, the team won the NL Central title. The Brewers reached the NL Championship Series but lost to the Cardinals.

The Brewers finished the 2018 season with 96 wins and beat the Cubs in a tiebreaker to win the **NL** Central. The team **swept** the Rockies in the NL **Division** Series but came just short of the World Series. Josh Hader powered a strong **bullpen**. The Brew Crew proved they still had plenty of fizz!

The Brewers made the playoffs a total of six times from 2019 to 2025. In 2024, they won the **NL Central** with a **walk-off** hit by Jake Bauers.

The 2025 season ended on a disappointing note when the Brewers lost to the Dodgers in the NL Championship Series. However, they had a **franchise-record** 97 wins in the regular season. Fans were excited for what was to come.

HALL OF FAME

Robin Yount spent his 20-year career with the Milwaukee Brewers. He collected 3,142 hits, won two **AL** MVP Awards, and helped lead the team to the 1982 World Series. Yount played both shortstop and center field and was known for his hustle and timely hitting. He was named to the Baseball Hall of Fame in 1999.

Miller
HALL
POSTSEASON 2008
BREWERS TEAM STORE
HARDY
POSTSEASON 2008
ROBIN YOUNT
"The Kid"
Milwaukee Brewers
1974-1993

Paul Molitor played for the Milwaukee Brewers from 1978 to 1992. He collected 2,281 hits, 160 home runs, and stole 412 bases. He helped the Brewers reach the 1982 World Series. Molitor entered the Hall of Fame in 2004.

Christian Yelich joined the Milwaukee Brewers in 2018 and quickly became a star. He won the **NL** MVP Award that year with 36 home runs, 110 **RBIs**, and a .326 batting average. In 2019, Yelich hit a career-high 44 home runs and stole 30 bases. He helped lead the Brewers to the playoffs and performs as one of the best hitters in the league.

GLOSSARY

American League (AL) – one of two 15-team leagues that make up MLB.

bullpen – the area of the field where relief pitchers warm up before entering a game.

division – a number of teams grouped together in a sport for competitive purposes.

franchise – a sports organization, including the top-level team and all minor league affiliates.

National League (NL) – one of two 15-team leagues that make up MLB.

pennant – the title achieved by the team that wins its division or league championship.

record – a top achievement by a team.

Runs Batted In (RBI) – a statistic that credits a batter for making a play that allows a run to be scored.

swept – to have won all games in a series.

walk-off – any victory in which the home team scores the winning run in the bottom of the final inning.

wild-card – a place or a team chosen to fill a place in a competition after the regularly qualified players or teams have all been decided.

ONLINE RESOURCES

To learn more about the Milwaukee Brewers, please visit abdobooklinks.com or scan this QR code. These links are routinely monitored and updated to provide the most current information available.

INDEX

365

DEVOCIONES PARA COMENZAR TU DÍA

BroadStreet
ESPAÑOL

BroadStreet Publishing Group, LLC
Savage, Minnesota, E.U.A.
BroadStreetPublishing.com

Jesús primero para hombres
Edición en español © 2025 por BroadStreet Publishing®
Publicado originalmente en inglés con el título *Jesus First for Men*,
© 2023 por BroadStreet Publishing®

ISBN: 978-1-4245-7077-5 (piel símil)
e-ISBN: 978-1-4245-7078-2 (libro electrónico)

Diseño por Chris Garborg | garborgdesign.com

Traducción, adaptación del diseño y corrección en español por LM Editorial Services | lmeditorial.com | lydia@lmeditorial.com con la colaboración de Belmonte Traductores (traducción) y www.produccioneditorial.com (tipografía)

Impreso en China / Printed in China

25 26 27 28 29 * 6 5 4 3 2 1